NEONATAL AND PEDIATRIC RESPIRATORY CARE

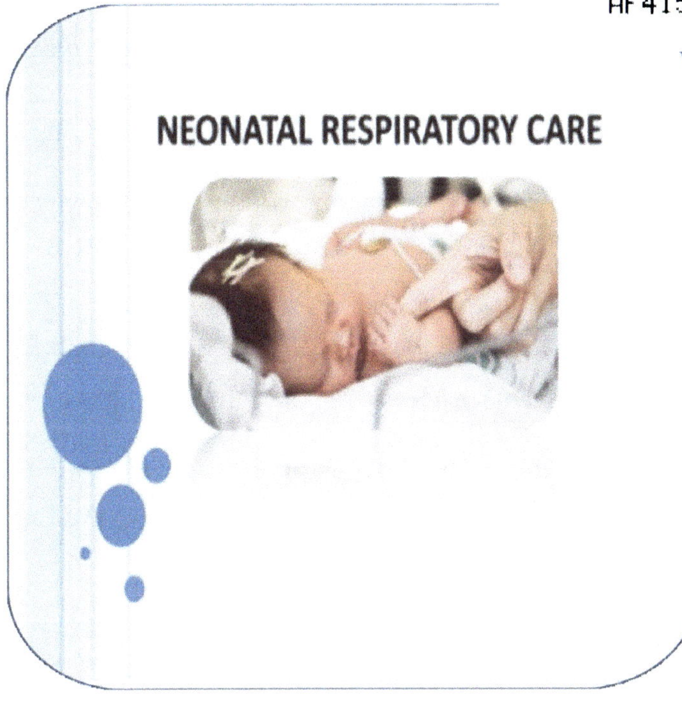

TABLE OF CONTENTS

COURSE OVERVIEW

This course provides a comprehensive exploration of neonatal and pediatric respiratory care, designed for healthcare professionals involved in the diagnosis, treatment, and management of respiratory conditions in young patients. Participants will gain in-depth knowledge of common and complex respiratory disorders, diagnostic techniques, management strategies, and the ethical and legal considerations unique to pediatric care.

COURSE OBJECTIVES

By the end of this course, participants will be able to Understand Pediatric Respiratory Physiology, Diagnose and Manage Respiratory Disorders, Implement Therapeutic Interventions, Address Acute Respiratory Distress, Manage Long-Term Care and Follow-Up, Navigate Ethical and Legal Issues, Integrate Multidisciplinary Approaches, Explore Future Directions and Innovations. This course aims to provide healthcare professionals with a thorough understanding of pediatric respiratory care, equipping them with the knowledge and skills to address both common and complex respiratory conditions effectively.

COURSE MATERIALS

To learn this course, **healthcare providers/ participants** must be provided with materials like a Pen, pencil, notebook, and notepad to better understand and make it easy for them to learn.

INTRODUCTION

Respiratory care is a critical component of healthcare, especially in the realms of neonatology and pediatrics. The delicate respiratory systems of newborns and young children require specialized knowledge and skills to ensure they receive the best possible care. This book, "Mastering Neonatal and Pediatric Respiratory Care: A Comprehensive Guide for Healthcare Providers," is designed to equip healthcare providers with the essential information and practical tools they need to excel in this challenging and rewarding field.

The primary goal of this book is to provide a thorough understanding of the respiratory systems of neonates and children, highlighting the unique aspects that differentiate them from adults. By focusing on the anatomical, physiological, and developmental differences, healthcare providers can better appreciate the specific needs and vulnerabilities of this population. This foundational knowledge is crucial for accurately diagnosing and effectively treating respiratory conditions in neonates and children.

"Mastering Neonatal and Pediatric Respiratory Care: A Comprehensive Guide for Healthcare Providers" is an invaluable resource for healthcare professionals dedicated to improving the respiratory health of neonates and children. Whether you are a seasoned practitioner or a student entering this field, this book will provide you with the knowledge, skills, and confidence to deliver exceptional care to your patients.

MODULE ONE

LESSON ONE: UNDERSTANDING NEONATAL AND PEDIATRIC RESPIRATORY ANATOMY

The respiratory system of neonates and children is uniquely different from that of adults, not only in size but also in function and development. To provide effective respiratory care, healthcare providers must have a thorough understanding of these differences. This lesson will explore the anatomical and physiological aspects of the neonatal and pediatric respiratory systems, emphasizing their implications for clinical practice.

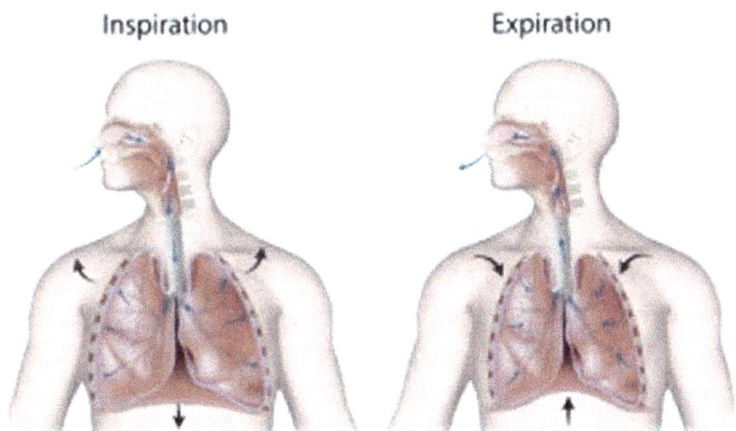

Anatomical Differences

One of the most significant differences between the respiratory systems of neonates and children compared to adults is the size and structure of their airways. Neonates and children have smaller airways, which are more susceptible to obstruction. The larynx in neonates is positioned higher in the neck, which affects the way they breathe and swallow. This anatomical feature also makes neonates more prone to airway obstruction during feeding and respiratory distress.

The trachea in neonates is shorter and narrower, increasing the risk of airway resistance and making intubation more challenging. The bronchi and bronchioles are also smaller and less rigid, which can lead to a higher susceptibility to collapse, especially in conditions that cause inflammation or secretions. Understanding these anatomical differences is crucial for recognizing signs of respiratory distress and choosing appropriate interventions.

Physiological Differences

Neonates and children also exhibit unique physiological characteristics that influence their respiratory function. One of the key differences is their higher metabolic rate, which results in increased oxygen consumption. This higher demand for oxygen makes neonates and children more vulnerable to hypoxia and respiratory failure. Additionally, the respiratory muscles of neonates, including the diaphragm and intercostal muscles, are less developed and more prone to fatigue.

The alveoli, where gas exchange occurs, are fewer in number at birth and continue to develop rapidly during the first few years of life. This ongoing development means that neonates and young children have a lower surface area for gas exchange compared to adults, making them more susceptible to respiratory compromise. The surfactant system, which reduces surface tension in the alveoli, is also immature in preterm infants, contributing to conditions such as respiratory distress syndrome.

Implications for Clinical Practice

Understanding these anatomical and physiological differences is essential for effective respiratory care in neonates and children.

Healthcare providers must be vigilant in monitoring for signs of respiratory distress, which can manifest differently than in adults. Symptoms such as nasal flaring, grunting, retractions, and cyanosis are critical indicators of respiratory compromise in this population.

When providing respiratory support, it is important to consider the size and developmental stage of the patient. Techniques such as intubation, mechanical ventilation, and the use of continuous positive airway pressure (CPAP) require careful adjustment to accommodate the smaller and more delicate airways of neonates and children. Additionally, the choice of respiratory equipment, such as masks and endotracheal tubes, must be appropriate for the patient's size and age.

A comprehensive understanding of the anatomical and physiological differences in the respiratory systems of neonates and children is fundamental for healthcare providers. This knowledge forms the basis for recognizing respiratory distress, choosing appropriate interventions, and providing effective care.

DISCUSSION QUESTIONS

How do the unique physiological characteristics of neonates and children influence the management of respiratory conditions compared to adults?

What are the potential complications that arise from the rapid growth and development of the respiratory system in children, and how should these be addressed in clinical practice?

LESSON TWO: COMMON RESPIRATORY CONDITIONS IN NEONATES AND CHILDREN

Respiratory conditions in neonates and children can range from mild to life-threatening. Understanding these conditions, their etiology, clinical presentation, and management is crucial for healthcare providers. This lesson will provide a comprehensive overview of the most common respiratory conditions encountered in neonatal and pediatric patients.

NEONATAL RESPIRATORY DISTRESS SYNDROME (NRDS)

- **Etiology and Pathophysiology**

Neonatal Respiratory Distress Syndrome (NRDS), also known as Hyaline Membrane Disease, primarily affects preterm infants. It is caused by a deficiency of surfactant, a substance that reduces surface tension within the alveoli, preventing collapse during exhalation. Surfactant deficiency leads to alveolar collapse, decreased lung compliance, and impaired gas exchange.

- **Clinical Presentation**

Infants with NRDS typically present with signs of respiratory distress shortly after birth, including tachypnea, nasal flaring, grunting, intercostal retractions, and cyanosis. Chest X-rays often show a ground-glass appearance with air bronchograms.

- **Management**

The management of NRDS includes the administration of exogenous surfactant, usually via endotracheal tube, and respiratory support. Continuous Positive Airway Pressure (CPAP) and mechanical ventilation may be necessary to maintain adequate oxygenation and ventilation. Prenatal corticosteroids administered to the mother can reduce the incidence and severity of NRDS in preterm infants.

BRONCHIOLITIS

- **Etiology and Pathophysiology**

Bronchiolitis is a common lower respiratory tract infection in infants and young children, most often caused by Respiratory Syncytial Virus (RSV). The infection leads to inflammation, edema, and mucus production in the bronchioles, causing obstruction and impaired gas exchange.

- **Clinical Presentation**

Children with bronchiolitis typically present with rhinorrhea, cough, wheezing, and respiratory distress. Physical examination may reveal tachypnea, retractions, nasal flaring, and crackles or wheezes on auscultation. Severe cases can result in apnea or respiratory failure.

- **Management**

Management of bronchiolitis is primarily supportive, including hydration, oxygen therapy, and suctioning of nasal secretions. In severe cases, hospitalization may be required for respiratory support with CPAP or mechanical ventilation. Pharmacological treatments such as bronchodilators and corticosteroids are generally not recommended due to limited efficacy.

ASTHMA

- **Etiology and Pathophysiology**

Asthma is a chronic inflammatory disorder of the airways characterized by recurrent episodes of wheezing, breathlessness, chest tightness, and coughing. In children, asthma can be triggered by allergens, viral infections, exercise, and environmental factors. The inflammation leads to airway hyperresponsiveness, bronchoconstriction, and mucus production.

- **Clinical Presentation**

Asthma in children presents with episodic symptoms including wheezing, coughing (often worse at night or early morning), shortness of breath, and chest tightness. Physical examination during an acute episode may reveal expiratory wheezing and prolonged expiration.

- **Management**

The management of asthma involves both acute and long-term strategies. Acute management includes the use of short-acting beta-agonists (e.g., albuterol) for rapid relief of bronchoconstriction. Long-term management focuses on controlling inflammation with inhaled corticosteroids, leukotriene modifiers, and long-acting beta-agonists. An asthma action plan and regular follow-up are essential for effective management.

PNEUMONIA

- **Etiology and Pathophysiology**

Pneumonia is an infection of the lungs that can be caused by bacteria, viruses, fungi, or parasites. In children, bacterial pathogens such as Streptococcus pneumoniae and Haemophilus influenzae are common causes. Viral pneumonia is often due to RSV, influenza, or adenovirus. The infection leads to inflammation and consolidation of lung tissue, impairing gas exchange.

- **Clinical Presentation**

Children with pneumonia may present with fever, cough, tachypnea, and difficulty breathing. Auscultation may reveal decreased breath sounds, crackles, or bronchial breath sounds. Chest X-rays typically show areas of consolidation.

- **Management**

Management of pneumonia depends on the etiological agent. Bacterial pneumonia is treated with appropriate antibiotics, while viral pneumonia is managed with supportive care including hydration and oxygen therapy. Severe cases may require hospitalization for intravenous antibiotics and respiratory support.

CYSTIC FIBROSIS

- **Etiology and Pathophysiology**

Cystic Fibrosis (CF) is a genetic disorder caused by mutations in the CFTR gene, leading to defective chloride transport and thick, sticky mucus production. This results in chronic respiratory infections, bronchiectasis, and progressive lung damage.

- **Clinical Presentation**

Children with CF often present with chronic cough, recurrent respiratory infections, wheezing, and failure to thrive. Physical examination may reveal digital clubbing, nasal polyps, and crackles or wheezes on auscultation.

- **Management**

Management of CF is multidisciplinary and includes airway clearance techniques, inhaled medications (e.g., bronchodilators, mucolytics), antibiotics for infections, and nutritional support. CF transmembrane conductance regulator (CFTR) modulators are a newer class of drugs that target the underlying defect in CF.

Understanding common respiratory conditions in neonates and children is essential for providing effective care. Each condition presents unique challenges and requires specific management strategies. By recognizing the signs and symptoms, utilizing appropriate diagnostic tools, and implementing evidence-based treatments, healthcare providers can significantly improve the respiratory health and outcomes of their pediatric patients.

DISCUSSION QUESTIONS

How can early identification and management of conditions such as RSV and bronchiolitis impact long-term respiratory health in children?

What are the key differences in the presentation and management of asthma in children compared to adults?

MODULE TWO

LESSON ONE: DIAGNOSTIC TECHNIQUES AND TOOLS

Accurate diagnosis of respiratory conditions in neonates and children is critical for effective management and treatment. This lesson will explore various diagnostic techniques and tools used to assess respiratory function and identify respiratory pathologies in this patient population. Understanding these diagnostic modalities will enable healthcare providers to make informed clinical decisions and tailor interventions to each patient's unique needs.

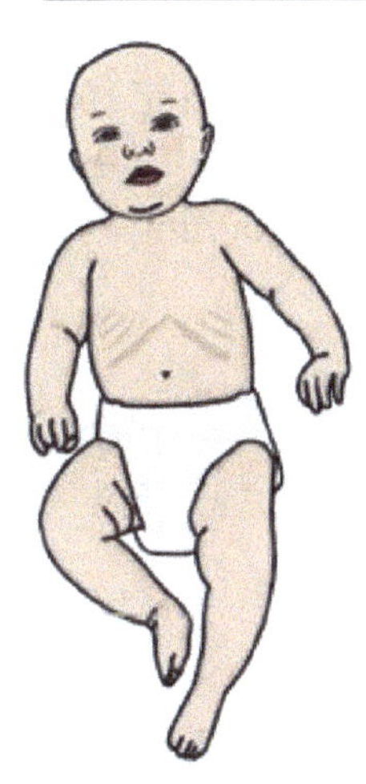

PHYSICAL EXAMINATION

Inspection

The physical examination begins with a thorough inspection of the patient. Key observations include:

- General Appearance: Assess for signs of respiratory distress such as cyanosis, nasal flaring, and use of accessory muscles.
- Breathing Pattern: Note the rate, rhythm, and effort of breathing. Tachypnea, bradypnea, or irregular breathing patterns can indicate underlying respiratory issues.
- Chest Movement: Look for asymmetry or paradoxical movements, which may suggest conditions such as pneumothorax or diaphragmatic paralysis.

Auscultation

Auscultation of the lungs is a vital component of the physical examination. Healthcare providers should listen for:

- Breath Sounds: Assess for normal breath sounds (vesicular) and any abnormal sounds such as crackles, wheezes, or diminished breath sounds.
- Adventitious Sounds: Crackles may indicate fluid in the alveoli (e.g., pneumonia or pulmonary edema), while wheezes suggest airway obstruction (e.g., asthma or bronchiolitis).

Palpation and Percussion

- Palpation: Assess for tenderness, subcutaneous emphysema, or masses. Tactile fremitus can help identify areas of consolidation or pleural effusion.
- Percussion: Percussion of the chest helps differentiate between areas of normal resonance and abnormal dullness or hyperresonance, indicating consolidation, effusion, or pneumothorax.

IMAGING STUDIES

Chest X-Ray

Chest X-rays are commonly used to evaluate respiratory conditions. They provide valuable information about the structure and pathology of the lungs, pleura, and surrounding tissues. Key findings on chest X-rays include:

- Consolidation: Indicates pneumonia or lung infection.
- Hyperinflation: Seen in conditions like asthma and bronchiolitis.
- Interstitial Patterns: Suggests viral infections or chronic lung disease.
- Pleural Effusion: Identified by blunting of the costophrenic angles and fluid levels.

Computed Tomography (CT) Scan

CT scans offer more detailed imaging of the lungs and thoracic structures compared to chest X-rays. They are particularly useful in diagnosing complex cases, such as congenital anomalies, interstitial lung diseases, and bronchiectasis. CT scans can identify small nodules, cysts, and detailed anatomical abnormalities.

LABORATORY TESTS

Blood Gas Analysis

Arterial blood gas (ABG) analysis is crucial for assessing oxygenation, ventilation, and acid-base status. Key parameters include:

- PaO2: Partial pressure of oxygen, indicating the effectiveness of oxygenation.
- PaCO2: Partial pressure of carbon dioxide, reflecting ventilatory status.
- pH: Indicates acid-base balance.
- HCO3-: Bicarbonate level, reflecting metabolic component of acid-base balance.

Complete Blood Count (CBC)

A CBC can provide insights into the patient's overall health and identify signs of infection or inflammation. Elevated white blood cell counts may indicate bacterial infections, while eosinophilia can suggest allergic conditions or parasitic infections.

C-Reactive Protein (CRP) and Procalcitonin

CRP and procalcitonin are inflammatory markers that can help differentiate between bacterial and viral infections. Elevated levels of these markers are more suggestive of bacterial infections and can guide antibiotic therapy decisions.

Pulmonary Function Tests (PFTs)

Pulmonary function tests are essential for assessing lung function, particularly in older children who can follow instructions. Key PFTs include:

- Spirometry: Measures the volume and flow of air during inhalation and exhalation. Key parameters include FEV1 (forced expiratory volume in one second) and FVC (forced vital capacity).
- Peak Expiratory Flow (PEF): Assesses the maximum speed of exhalation, useful for monitoring asthma control.

Bronchoscopy

Bronchoscopy is an invasive procedure that allows direct visualization of the airways using a flexible or rigid bronchoscope. It is used for diagnostic and therapeutic purposes, including:

- Biopsy: Obtaining tissue samples for histopathological examination.
- Bronchoalveolar Lavage (BAL): Collecting samples from the lower respiratory tract for microbiological analysis.
- Foreign Body Removal: Extracting inhaled foreign objects.

NON-INVASIVE MONITORING

Pulse Oximetry

Pulse oximetry is a non-invasive method for monitoring oxygen saturation (SpO_2) in the blood. It is useful for continuous monitoring of oxygenation status in neonates and children, particularly in critical care settings.

Capnography

Capnography measures the concentration of carbon dioxide (CO_2) in exhaled air, providing real-time information about ventilation status. It is valuable in monitoring patients under sedation, during mechanical ventilation, and in emergency situations.

Accurate diagnosis of respiratory conditions in neonates and children relies on a combination of thorough physical examination, imaging studies, laboratory tests, pulmonary function tests, and specialized procedures such as bronchoscopy. Mastering these diagnostic techniques and tools is essential for healthcare providers to deliver effective and tailored respiratory care. By integrating clinical findings with diagnostic results, healthcare providers can make informed decisions and optimize patient outcomes.

DISCUSSION QUESTIONS

How do non-invasive diagnostic techniques like pulse oximetry and capnography enhance the management of respiratory conditions in neonates and children?

What are the limitations of conventional imaging techniques, such as chest X-rays and CT scans, in diagnosing respiratory disorders in pediatric patients?

LESSON TWO: RESPIRATORY THERAPEUTICS AND INTERVENTIONS

Effective management of respiratory conditions in neonates and children requires a comprehensive understanding of various therapeutic strategies and interventions. This lesson will explore pharmacological and non-pharmacological treatments, highlighting evidence-based practices and emerging trends. By mastering these therapeutic approaches, healthcare providers can ensure optimal care for their young patients.

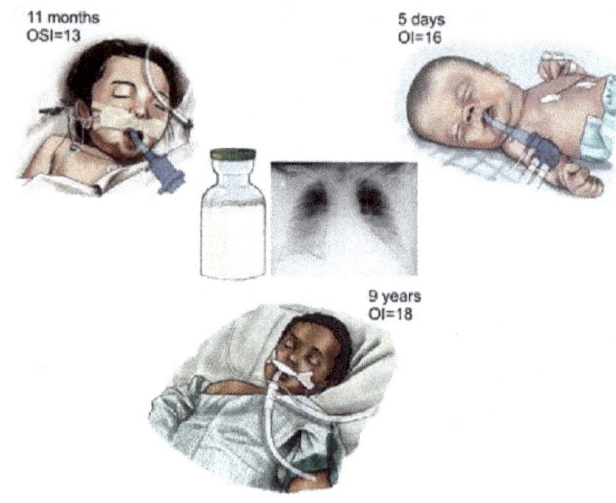

PHARMACOLOGICAL TREATMENTS

Bronchodilators

Bronchodilators are medications that relax the smooth muscles of the airways, improving airflow and alleviating symptoms of bronchoconstriction. They are commonly used in conditions such as asthma and bronchiolitis.

- Short-Acting Beta-Agonists (SABAs): Medications like albuterol and levalbuterol provide rapid relief of acute bronchoconstriction. They are typically administered via inhalers or nebulizers.

- Long-Acting Beta-Agonists (LABAs): Drugs such as salmeterol and formoterol are used for long-term control of asthma. They are often combined with inhaled corticosteroids (ICS) to enhance efficacy.

Inhaled Corticosteroids (ICS)

ICS are the cornerstone of asthma management, reducing airway inflammation and hyperresponsiveness. Common ICS include budesonide, fluticasone, and beclomethasone. These medications are administered via inhalers and are effective in preventing asthma exacerbations.

Systemic Corticosteroids

Systemic corticosteroids, such as prednisone and methylprednisolone, are used in severe asthma exacerbations and other acute inflammatory respiratory conditions. They reduce inflammation and improve symptoms but are typically limited to short-term use due to potential side effects.

Antibiotics

Antibiotics are essential for treating bacterial respiratory infections such as pneumonia and bacterial tracheitis. The choice of antibiotic depends on the suspected pathogen and local resistance patterns. Commonly used antibiotics include amoxicillin, azithromycin, and ceftriaxone.

Antivirals

Antiviral medications, such as oseltamivir, are used to treat influenza infections in children. Early administration can reduce the severity and duration of symptoms. Ribavirin is another antiviral used for severe RSV infections, particularly in high-risk infants.

Mucolytics and Expectorants

Mucolytics and expectorants help reduce mucus viscosity and promote clearance from the airways. Medications like guaifenesin and acetylcysteine are commonly used in conditions with excessive mucus production, such as cystic fibrosis and chronic bronchitis.

Leukotriene Modifiers

Leukotriene modifiers, such as montelukast and zafirlukast, are used in asthma management to reduce inflammation and bronchoconstriction. They are particularly useful for patients with allergic asthma and exercise-induced bronchoconstriction.

NON-PHARMACOLOGICAL INTERVENTIONS

Oxygen Therapy

Oxygen therapy is a critical intervention for managing hypoxemia in neonates and children. Various methods of oxygen delivery include:

- Nasal Cannula: Provides low-flow oxygen and is suitable for mild to moderate hypoxemia.
- Simple Mask: Delivers higher concentrations of oxygen than a nasal cannula.
- Non-Rebreather Mask: Used for severe hypoxemia, delivering high concentrations of oxygen.
- High-Flow Nasal Cannula (HFNC): Provides heated and humidified high-flow oxygen, improving oxygenation and reducing work of breathing.

Continuous Positive Airway Pressure (CPAP)

CPAP is used to maintain airway patency and improve oxygenation in conditions such as NRDS and obstructive sleep apnea. It delivers a constant positive pressure to the airways, preventing collapse and enhancing gas exchange.

Mechanical Ventilation

Mechanical ventilation is necessary for patients with severe respiratory failure who cannot maintain adequate oxygenation and ventilation. Modes of mechanical ventilation include:

- Volume-Controlled Ventilation: Delivers a preset tidal volume with each breath.
- Pressure-Controlled Ventilation: Delivers breaths at a preset pressure.
- Synchronized Intermittent Mandatory Ventilation (SIMV): Combines mandatory breaths with spontaneous breathing.

Surfactant Replacement Therapy

Surfactant replacement therapy is essential for managing NRDS in preterm infants. Exogenous surfactant is administered via endotracheal tube to reduce surface tension in the alveoli, improving lung compliance and gas exchange.

Airway Clearance Techniques

Airway clearance techniques are vital for patients with conditions that lead to excessive mucus production, such as cystic fibrosis. Techniques include:

- Chest Physiotherapy (CPT): Manual percussion and vibration to loosen mucus.
- Positive Expiratory Pressure (PEP) Therapy: Devices that create resistance during exhalation, helping to clear mucus.
- High-Frequency Chest Wall Oscillation (HFCWO): Vests that deliver rapid oscillations to mobilize secretions.

Humidification and Hydration

Humidification of inspired air is essential to prevent drying of the airways, especially in patients receiving oxygen therapy. Adequate hydration also helps to thin mucus secretions, facilitating clearance.

EMERGING THERAPIES

Gene Therapy

Gene therapy is a promising approach for treating genetic respiratory disorders such as cystic fibrosis. By correcting the underlying genetic defect, gene therapy has the potential to provide long-term benefits and improve quality of life.

Monoclonal Antibodies

Monoclonal antibodies, such as palivizumab, are used for the prophylaxis of severe RSV infections in high-risk infants. These antibodies target specific viral proteins, preventing infection and reducing disease severity.

Stem Cell Therapy

Stem cell therapy is an emerging field with potential applications in repairing and regenerating damaged lung tissue. Research is ongoing to explore the efficacy and safety of stem cell therapy in various respiratory conditions.

Respiratory therapeutics and interventions in neonates and children require a multifaceted approach, combining pharmacological and non-pharmacological strategies. By staying informed about evidence-based practices and emerging therapies, healthcare providers can deliver optimal care and improve respiratory outcomes for their patients. Mastery of these therapeutic approaches is essential for addressing the unique challenges of respiratory care in this vulnerable population.

DISCUSSION QUESTIONS

What are the benefits and challenges associated with the use of high-frequency oscillatory ventilation in the treatment of neonatal respiratory distress syndrome?

How does the use of non-invasive ventilation techniques, such as CPAP, impact the management of pediatric respiratory conditions?

MODULE THREE

LESSON ONE: RESPIRATORY MONITORING AND SUPPORT IN CRITICAL CARE

Effective respiratory monitoring and support are vital in the critical care management of neonates and children with severe respiratory conditions. This lesson delves into the advanced monitoring techniques and support strategies used in the pediatric intensive care unit (PICU) to ensure optimal respiratory function and patient outcomes.

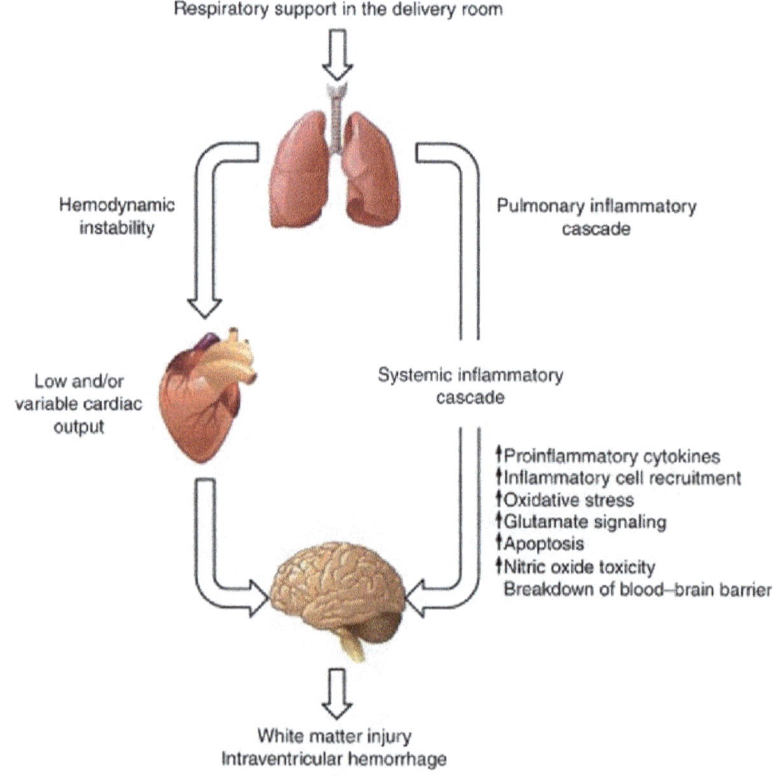

RESPIRATORY MONITORING

Vital Signs Monitoring

Continuous monitoring of vital signs is fundamental in critically ill patients. Key parameters include:

- Heart Rate: Tachycardia can indicate respiratory distress, while bradycardia may signal severe hypoxemia or impending respiratory failure.
- Respiratory Rate: Elevated respiratory rate (tachypnea) often accompanies respiratory distress; a sudden drop can indicate fatigue and impending respiratory failure.
- Blood Pressure: Hypotension can be a sign of sepsis or shock, impacting respiratory function.
- Oxygen Saturation (SpO2): Monitored using pulse oximetry to assess oxygenation status and guide oxygen therapy.

Blood Gas Analysis

Arterial blood gas (ABG) analysis provides critical information on oxygenation, ventilation, and acid-base balance. Regular ABG measurements help guide ventilation strategies and assess the effectiveness of interventions.

- pH: Reflects acid-base balance; acidosis or alkalosis requires correction.
- PaO2: Indicates arterial oxygenation; hypoxemia requires intervention.
- PaCO2: Reflects ventilation status; hypercapnia indicates inadequate ventilation.
- HCO3-: Shows metabolic component of acid-base status.

Capnography

Capnography measures the concentration of carbon dioxide (CO_2) in exhaled air, providing real-time information about ventilation. It is particularly useful in monitoring mechanically ventilated patients and during procedural sedation.

- End-Tidal CO_2 (EtCO2): Reflects the amount of CO_2 at the end of exhalation, helping to assess ventilation efficiency and detect apnea or hypoventilation early.

RESPIRATORY SUPPORT STRATEGIES

Non-Invasive Ventilation (NIV)

Non-invasive ventilation provides respiratory support without the need for endotracheal intubation. It is effective in conditions like acute respiratory distress and chronic respiratory failure.

- Continuous Positive Airway Pressure (CPAP): Delivers constant positive pressure to keep airways open, used in conditions like obstructive sleep apnea and NRDS.
- Bi-Level Positive Airway Pressure (BiPAP): Provides different pressure levels for inhalation and exhalation, useful in conditions like COPD exacerbations and acute asthma.

Invasive Mechanical Ventilation

Invasive mechanical ventilation is necessary for patients who cannot maintain adequate oxygenation and ventilation. It involves endotracheal intubation and the use of ventilators to support breathing.

- Volume-Controlled Ventilation: Delivers a preset tidal volume with each breath, ensuring consistent ventilation.
- Pressure-Controlled Ventilation: Delivers breaths at a preset pressure, protecting the lungs from over-distension.
- High-Frequency Oscillatory Ventilation (HFOV): Uses very high respiratory rates and small tidal volumes to minimize lung injury while ensuring adequate gas exchange.

Extracorporeal Membrane Oxygenation (ECMO)

ECMO is a life-saving technique for patients with severe respiratory or cardiac failure unresponsive to conventional treatments. It involves the use of an external machine to oxygenate the blood and remove CO_2, allowing the lungs and heart to rest and recover.

- Veno-Venous ECMO (VV-ECMO): Used primarily for severe respiratory failure.
- Veno-Arterial ECMO (VA-ECMO): Used for both respiratory and cardiac failure.

ADVANCED MONITORING TECHNIQUES

Respiratory Mechanics Monitoring

Monitoring respiratory mechanics helps optimize ventilator settings and prevent lung injury. Key parameters include:

- Compliance: Reflects lung elasticity; reduced compliance indicates stiff lungs, as seen in ARDS.
- Resistance: Indicates airway resistance; increased resistance suggests airway obstruction.
- Work of Breathing: Assesses the effort required to breathe; high work of breathing indicates respiratory distress.

Imaging Studies

Regular imaging studies, such as chest X-rays and ultrasound, are essential for monitoring lung conditions and guiding interventions.

- Chest X-Ray: Helps assess lung expansion, detect pneumothorax, atelectasis, or pleural effusion, and monitor endotracheal tube placement.
- Lung Ultrasound: Non-invasive technique to detect pleural effusion, consolidation, and pneumothorax.

Sedation and Pain Management

Effective sedation and pain management are crucial in critically ill pediatric patients to ensure comfort and reduce stress, which can exacerbate respiratory distress.

- Sedatives: Medications such as midazolam and dexmedetomidine are used for sedation in mechanically ventilated patients.
- Analgesics: Opioids like morphine and fentanyl are commonly used for pain relief.

Weaning and Extubation

Weaning from mechanical ventilation and successful extubation require careful assessment and planning to ensure the patient can maintain adequate respiratory function independently.

- Weaning Protocols: Gradual reduction of ventilatory support while monitoring respiratory parameters and patient response.
- Spontaneous Breathing Trials (SBTs): Assess the patient's ability to breathe independently before extubation.
- Post-Extubation Care: Close monitoring and support to address any respiratory compromise post-extubation.

Respiratory monitoring and support in critical care require a multidisciplinary approach and advanced techniques to ensure optimal outcomes for neonates and children with severe respiratory conditions. By utilizing a combination of non-invasive and invasive strategies, continuous monitoring, and appropriate interventions, healthcare providers can manage respiratory distress and failure effectively. Mastery of these techniques is essential for providing high-quality care in the PICU and improving the survival and quality of life of critically ill pediatric patients.

DISCUSSION QUESTIONS

What are the key considerations in deciding whether to use invasive versus non-invasive ventilation methods in critically ill pediatric patients?

How can early intervention strategies be optimized to prevent the progression of acute respiratory distress in neonates and children?

MODULE FOUR

LESSON ONE: PREVENTIVE MEASURES AND PUBLIC HEALTH STRATEGIES

Prevention is a cornerstone of pediatric respiratory care, aimed at reducing the incidence and severity of respiratory illnesses. This lesson explores various preventive measures and public health strategies that healthcare providers can implement to safeguard the respiratory health of neonates and children. These strategies range from vaccination and infection control to environmental interventions and health education.

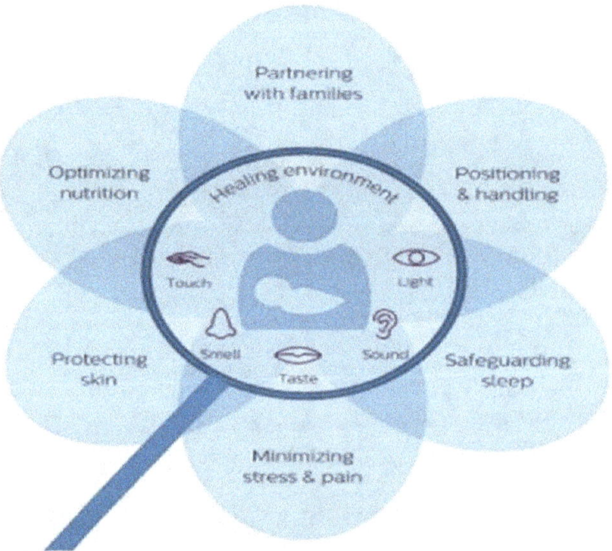

VACCINATION

Routine Immunizations

Vaccination is one of the most effective methods for preventing respiratory infections. Key vaccines include:

- Influenza Vaccine: Annual vaccination is recommended for all children aged six months and older. The influenza vaccine reduces the incidence of flu-related respiratory illnesses and complications.
- Pneumococcal Vaccine: The pneumococcal conjugate vaccine (PCV) protects against Streptococcus pneumoniae, a common cause of pneumonia, meningitis, and sepsis in children.
- Pertussis Vaccine: Part of the DTaP (diphtheria, tetanus, and pertussis) vaccine series, this vaccine protects against whooping cough, a highly contagious respiratory disease.

RSV Prophylaxis

Respiratory Syncytial Virus (RSV) is a major cause of bronchiolitis and pneumonia in infants. High-risk infants, such as those born prematurely or with congenital heart disease, may benefit from RSV prophylaxis with palivizumab, a monoclonal antibody administered monthly during RSV season.

INFECTION CONTROL PRACTICES

Hand Hygiene

Hand hygiene is a simple yet effective measure to prevent the spread of respiratory infections. Healthcare providers should adhere to strict hand hygiene practices, including handwashing with soap and water or using alcohol-based hand sanitizers, especially before and after patient contact.

Respiratory Hygiene

Promoting respiratory hygiene practices, such as covering the mouth and nose with a tissue or elbow when coughing or sneezing, can reduce the transmission of respiratory pathogens. Educating children and caregivers on these practices is essential.

Isolation Precautions

Implementing isolation precautions for patients with contagious respiratory infections can prevent the spread within healthcare settings. This includes using personal protective equipment (PPE), such as masks, gowns, and gloves, and placing patients in private rooms or cohorting them with others who have the same infection.

ENVIRONMENTAL INTERVENTIONS

Air Quality Control

Improving indoor air quality can significantly reduce respiratory problems in children. Strategies include:

- Eliminating Tobacco Smoke: Exposure to secondhand smoke is a major risk factor for respiratory illnesses. Banning smoking in homes and cars can protect children from harmful smoke exposure.
- Reducing Indoor Pollutants: Using air purifiers, maintaining proper ventilation, and avoiding the use of harsh chemicals can help improve indoor air quality.
- Controlling Outdoor Air Pollution: Advocating for policies that reduce industrial emissions and vehicle exhaust can improve overall air quality and respiratory health.

Allergy Control

Managing environmental allergens is crucial for children with asthma and allergic rhinitis. Measures include:

- Dust Mite Control: Using allergen-proof mattress and pillow covers, washing bedding in hot water, and reducing household dust can help control dust mite exposure.
- Pet Allergen Management: Limiting pet access to bedrooms and using air purifiers can reduce pet dander exposure.

- Mold Prevention: Controlling humidity levels and addressing water leaks promptly can prevent mold growth.

HEALTH EDUCATION

Asthma Action Plans

Developing and implementing individualized asthma action plans can help manage asthma effectively. These plans should include information on daily medications, how to recognize and handle worsening symptoms, and when to seek emergency care. Educating parents and caregivers on how to use these plans is crucial.

Smoking Cessation Programs

Supporting smoking cessation programs for parents and caregivers can significantly reduce children's exposure to secondhand smoke. Healthcare providers can offer resources and counseling to assist with quitting smoking.

Breastfeeding Promotion

Promoting and supporting breastfeeding can enhance the immune system of infants and reduce the risk of respiratory infections. Breastfeeding provides essential antibodies and nutrients that protect against pathogens.

COMMUNITY HEALTH INITIATIVES

School-Based Programs

Implementing health programs in schools can promote respiratory health. These programs can include vaccination clinics, asthma education, and initiatives to improve air quality within school buildings.

Public Awareness Campaigns

Raising public awareness about the importance of respiratory health through media campaigns, community events, and educational materials can encourage preventive practices. Topics can include the importance of vaccinations, hand hygiene, and avoiding exposure to tobacco smoke.

Access to Healthcare

Ensuring access to healthcare services, including regular check-ups, vaccinations, and timely treatment for respiratory conditions, is essential. Community health programs that provide affordable healthcare and reach underserved populations can improve overall respiratory health outcomes.

Preventive measures and public health strategies play a vital role in reducing the burden of respiratory illnesses in neonates and children. By implementing vaccination programs, infection control practices, environmental interventions, and health education, healthcare providers can create a safer and healthier environment for children. Community health initiatives and public awareness campaigns further enhance these efforts, promoting respiratory health on a broader scale. Mastery of these preventive strategies is essential for healthcare providers dedicated to improving pediatric respiratory care.

DISCUSSION QUESTIONS

What are the best practices for managing chronic respiratory conditions in children, and how can these practices be tailored to individual needs?

How can healthcare providers effectively monitor and address the impact of chronic respiratory conditions on a child's growth and development?

MODULE FIVE

LESSON ONE: SPECIAL CONSIDERATIONS IN NEONATAL AND PEDIATRIC RESPIRATORY CARE

The respiratory care of neonates and children presents unique challenges that require specialized knowledge and approaches. This lesson addresses special considerations in the respiratory management of this vulnerable population, including congenital anomalies, chronic respiratory conditions, and the impact of growth and development on respiratory health.

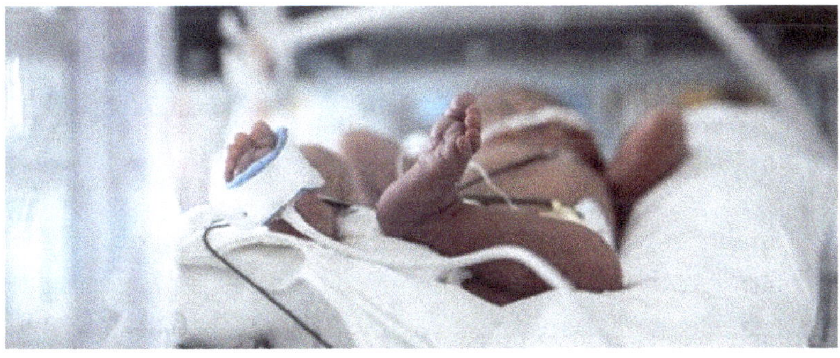

CONGENITAL RESPIRATORY ANOMALIES

Congenital Diaphragmatic Hernia (CDH)

CDH is a congenital defect characterized by the herniation of abdominal organs into the thoracic cavity due to a defect in the diaphragm. This condition can significantly impair lung development and function.

- Diagnosis: Prenatal ultrasound often identifies CDH, and postnatal diagnosis is confirmed with chest X-rays and clinical examination.

- Management: Initial stabilization involves respiratory support with mechanical ventilation or ECMO in severe cases. Surgical repair of the diaphragmatic defect is required to reposition the abdominal organs and allow for lung expansion.

Tracheoesophageal Fistula (TEF)

TEF is an abnormal connection between the trachea and esophagus, often associated with esophageal atresia. This condition can lead to severe respiratory distress and aspiration.

- Diagnosis: Symptoms include excessive drooling, coughing, and cyanosis during feeding. Radiographic studies with contrast can confirm the diagnosis.
- Management: Surgical correction is necessary to separate the trachea and esophagus and restore normal anatomy.

Laryngomalacia

Laryngomalacia is a common congenital anomaly where the laryngeal structures are abnormally soft, leading to airway obstruction and stridor.

- Diagnosis: Flexible laryngoscopy can visualize the floppy laryngeal tissues.
- Management: Most cases resolve spontaneously by 18 to 24 months of age. Severe cases may require surgical intervention, such as supraglottoplasty.

CHRONIC RESPIRATORY CONDITIONS

Asthma

Asthma is a chronic inflammatory condition characterized by airway hyperresponsiveness, bronchoconstriction, and mucus production.

- Diagnosis: Based on clinical history, spirometry, and response to bronchodilators.

- Management: Long-term control involves the use of inhaled corticosteroids, leukotriene modifiers, and bronchodilators. Education on avoiding triggers and using asthma action plans is crucial.

Cystic Fibrosis (CF)

CF is a genetic disorder affecting the respiratory and digestive systems, characterized by thick, sticky mucus production that leads to chronic respiratory infections and bronchiectasis.

- Diagnosis: Newborn screening, sweat chloride test, and genetic testing confirm CF.
- Management: Includes airway clearance techniques, mucolytics, antibiotics for infections, pancreatic enzyme replacement, and nutritional support. CF care requires a multidisciplinary approach.

Bronchopulmonary Dysplasia (BPD)

BPD is a chronic lung disease that affects premature infants who have required prolonged mechanical ventilation and oxygen therapy.

- Diagnosis: Based on a history of prematurity, prolonged respiratory support, and characteristic findings on chest X-rays.
- Management: Involves optimizing respiratory support, minimizing oxygen exposure, using diuretics and bronchodilators, and providing adequate nutrition to support lung growth and development.

IMPACT OF GROWTH AND DEVELOPMENT

Respiratory Physiology in Neonates

Neonates have unique respiratory physiology that differs from older children and adults. Their chest wall is more compliant, and they have higher metabolic rates, leading to increased oxygen consumption.

- Challenges: Neonates are more prone to respiratory fatigue, atelectasis, and hypoxemia.
- Care Strategies: Gentle ventilation strategies, careful monitoring, and prompt intervention are crucial in neonatal respiratory care.

Developmental Changes in Respiratory System

As children grow, their respiratory system undergoes significant changes. These include increases in lung volume, airway diameter, and the development of respiratory muscles.

- Considerations: Respiratory conditions may present differently at various ages, and treatment approaches must be tailored accordingly.
- Monitoring: Regular assessment of growth and development, along with pulmonary function tests, helps guide management.

PSYCHOSOCIAL ASPECTS OF CHRONIC RESPIRATORY CONDITIONS

Impact on Quality of Life

Chronic respiratory conditions can significantly impact the quality of life of children and their families. This includes limitations on physical activity, frequent hospitalizations, and the psychological burden of managing a chronic illness.

- Support Strategies: Providing psychological support, counseling, and connecting families with support groups can help manage the psychosocial impact.

Education and Empowerment

Educating families about the nature of respiratory conditions, treatment plans, and self-management strategies is essential.

Empowering families with knowledge and skills can improve adherence to treatment and overall outcomes.

- Tools: Providing written action plans, educational materials, and training on inhaler techniques and airway clearance methods.

Transition to Adult Care

As children with chronic respiratory conditions grow older, transitioning to adult care is a critical step. This process should be gradual and well-planned to ensure continuity of care.

- Planning: Begins in adolescence, involving both pediatric and adult care teams.
- Education: Focuses on self-management skills, understanding the disease, and preparing for adult healthcare responsibilities.

Special considerations in neonatal and pediatric respiratory care encompass a wide range of challenges, from managing congenital anomalies and chronic conditions to addressing the impact of growth and development. Understanding these unique aspects is essential for healthcare providers to deliver comprehensive and effective respiratory care. By focusing on individualized care plans, psychosocial support, and smooth transitions to adult care, providers can improve the quality of life and outcomes for children with respiratory conditions.

DISCUSSION QUESTIONS

What are the ethical considerations when deciding on the extent of intervention for neonates with severe congenital respiratory anomalies?

How can multidisciplinary teams effectively address the complex needs of children with chronic respiratory conditions like cystic fibrosis or bronchopulmonary dysplasia?

MODULE SIX

LESSON ONE: FUTURE DIRECTIONS AND INNOVATIONS IN NEONATAL AND PEDIATRIC RESPIRATORY CARE

The field of neonatal and pediatric respiratory care is continually evolving, driven by advances in technology, research, and a deeper understanding of respiratory physiology and pathology. This lesson explores the future directions and innovations that are poised to transform respiratory care for neonates and children, highlighting emerging technologies, novel therapies, and research trends.

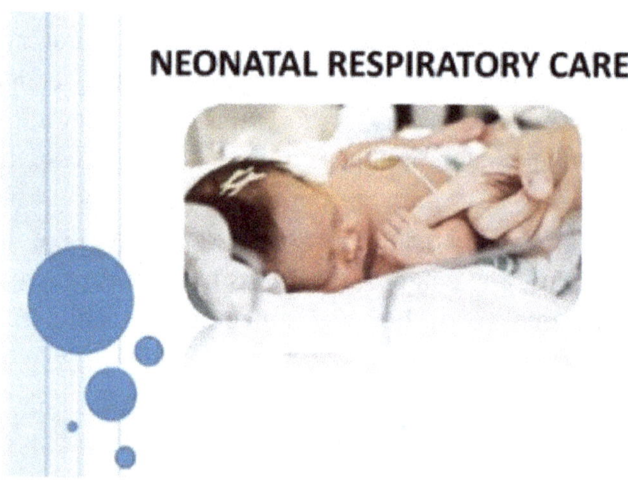

EMERGING TECHNOLOGIES

Artificial Intelligence and Machine Learning

Artificial intelligence (AI) and machine learning (ML) are revolutionizing healthcare by enabling more precise diagnostics, predictive analytics, and personalized treatment plans.

- Predictive Analytics: AI algorithms can analyze large datasets to predict respiratory events, such as asthma exacerbations or respiratory failure, allowing for timely interventions.
- Personalized Medicine: ML models can tailor treatment plans based on individual patient data, optimizing outcomes and minimizing side effects.
- Enhanced Diagnostics: AI-driven image analysis can improve the accuracy of diagnosing conditions like pneumonia, bronchopulmonary dysplasia, and congenital anomalies from radiographic images.

Telemedicine and Remote Monitoring

Telemedicine and remote monitoring technologies are expanding access to care, particularly for patients in remote or underserved areas.

- Virtual Consultations: Enable healthcare providers to assess and manage respiratory conditions without requiring in-person visits.
- Remote Monitoring Devices: Devices such as pulse oximeters, spirometers, and capnographs can transmit data in real-time to healthcare providers, facilitating continuous monitoring and early detection of issues.

NOVEL THERAPIES

Gene Therapy

Gene therapy holds promise for treating genetic respiratory disorders, such as cystic fibrosis, by correcting the underlying genetic defect.

- CFTR Modulators: Newer gene-editing technologies, such as CRISPR-Cas9, are being explored to correct mutations in the CFTR gene responsible for cystic fibrosis.
- Clinical Trials: Ongoing clinical trials are assessing the safety and efficacy of gene therapies in pediatric patients, with the potential for long-term benefits and improved quality of life.

Stem Cell Therapy

Stem cell therapy is an emerging field with potential applications in repairing and regenerating damaged lung tissue.

- Mesenchymal Stem Cells (MSCs): Research is exploring the use of MSCs for their anti-inflammatory and regenerative properties in conditions like bronchopulmonary dysplasia and acute respiratory distress syndrome (ARDS).
- Future Applications: Continued research may lead to new treatments that enhance lung repair and function in chronic respiratory conditions.

RESEARCH TRENDS

Precision Medicine

Precision medicine aims to tailor treatments to individual patients based on genetic, environmental, and lifestyle factors.

- Biomarker Research: Identifying biomarkers for different respiratory conditions can help predict disease progression, treatment response, and outcomes.
- Pharmacogenomics: Studying how genetic variations affect drug response can lead to more effective and personalized treatments.

Immunotherapy

Immunotherapy is being explored as a potential treatment for respiratory conditions characterized by inflammation and immune dysregulation.

- Biologics: Monoclonal antibodies targeting specific inflammatory pathways, such as interleukin-5 (IL-5) and immunoglobulin E (IgE), are being developed for conditions like asthma and eosinophilic esophagitis.

- Vaccines: Research is ongoing to develop vaccines against respiratory pathogens, such as RSV and influenza, with improved efficacy and longer-lasting protection.

INNOVATIONS IN RESPIRATORY SUPPORT

Advanced Ventilation Techniques

Innovations in mechanical ventilation aim to improve outcomes and reduce lung injury in critically ill neonates and children.

- Neurally Adjusted Ventilatory Assist (NAVA): This mode of ventilation uses the patient's neural respiratory drive to control ventilator support, potentially reducing the risk of lung injury and improving synchrony.
- High-Frequency Percussive Ventilation (HFPV): Combines high-frequency ventilation with percussive breaths, enhancing secretion clearance and improving oxygenation.

Extracorporeal Life Support

Advances in extracorporeal life support technologies are expanding their use in pediatric respiratory care.

- Portable ECMO Devices: Development of portable ECMO devices allows for more flexible and accessible use in various clinical settings, including transport and mobile units.
- Hybrid ECMO Systems: Combining ECMO with other support modalities, such as continuous renal replacement therapy (CRRT), for comprehensive care in multi-organ failure.

ETHICAL CONSIDERATIONS

Access to Innovations

Ensuring equitable access to advanced therapies and technologies is a critical ethical consideration.

- Healthcare Disparities: Addressing disparities in healthcare access and outcomes requires concerted efforts to provide innovative treatments to all patients, regardless of socioeconomic status or geographic location.
- Global Health Initiatives: Promoting global health initiatives and collaborations can help bring advanced respiratory care to underserved populations worldwide.

Informed Consent and Patient Autonomy

As new treatments and technologies emerge, maintaining transparency and respecting patient autonomy are paramount.

- Informed Consent: Ensuring that patients and families fully understand the benefits, risks, and uncertainties associated with novel therapies is essential for informed decision-making.
- Patient-Centered Care: Emphasizing patient-centered care and shared decision-making fosters trust and supports the ethical implementation of new treatments.

The future of neonatal and pediatric respiratory care is bright, with numerous innovations and advancements on the horizon. Emerging technologies, novel therapies, and ongoing research are set to transform the field, offering new hope and improved outcomes for young patients. Healthcare providers must stay abreast of these developments, integrate them into clinical practice, and address the ethical considerations that accompany these advancements. By embracing innovation and maintaining a patient-centered approach, the field of pediatric respiratory care can continue to evolve and improve the lives of children worldwide.

DISCUSSION QUESTIONS

What role do artificial intelligence and machine learning play in advancing the diagnosis and management of pediatric respiratory conditions?

How can emerging therapies, such as gene therapy and stem cell therapy, potentially transform the treatment landscape for chronic respiratory diseases in children?

MODULE SEVEN

LESSON ONE: ETHICAL AND LEGAL ISSUES IN NEONATAL AND PEDIATRIC RESPIRATORY CARE

Navigating the ethical and legal landscape in neonatal and pediatric respiratory care is complex, given the vulnerable nature of the patient population and the critical decisions that often need to be made. This lesson delves into key ethical principles, legal considerations, and the importance of effective communication in making informed and compassionate decisions.

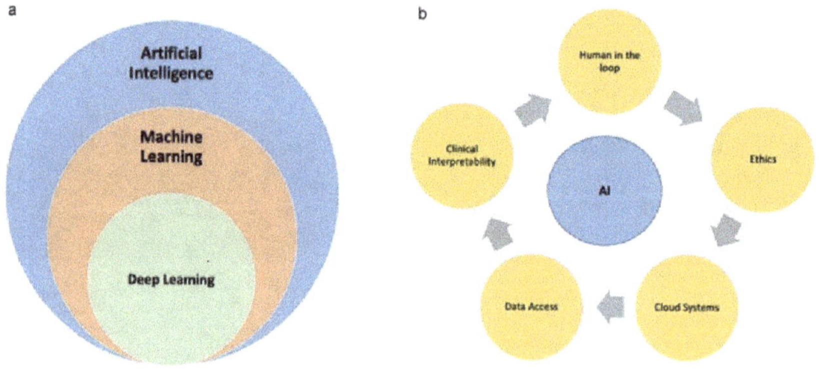

ETHICAL PRINCIPLES

Autonomy

Autonomy refers to respecting the patient's and family's right to make informed decisions about their care.

- Informed Consent: Ensuring that parents or guardians fully understand the risks, benefits, and alternatives of proposed

44

treatments is crucial. This involves clear communication and providing comprehensive information.

- Assent in Pediatrics: While young children cannot provide legal consent, involving older children in decision-making processes (assent) respects their developing autonomy and can improve cooperation and outcomes.

Beneficence and Non-Maleficence

These principles focus on doing good (beneficence) and avoiding harm (non-maleficence).

- Risk-Benefit Analysis: Healthcare providers must weigh the potential benefits of treatments against the risks, striving to maximize positive outcomes and minimize harm.
- Palliative Care: For conditions where curative treatment is not possible, palliative care focuses on providing comfort and improving the quality of life, adhering to these ethical principles.

Justice

Justice involves ensuring fair and equitable access to healthcare resources and treatments.

- Resource Allocation: Decisions about resource allocation, especially in critical care settings, must be made transparently and based on ethical guidelines to ensure fairness.
- Addressing Disparities: Efforts to reduce healthcare disparities, such as ensuring access to advanced therapies and preventive care for all children, align with the principle of justice.

LEGAL CONSIDERATIONS

Consent and Decision-Making

Legal aspects of consent and decision-making in pediatric care are
critical, given that children cannot legally consent to their own
treatment.

- Parental Authority: Parents or legal guardians typically have
  the authority to make medical decisions for their children.
  However, healthcare providers must ensure that these
  decisions are in the best interest of the child.
- Court Involvement: In cases of disagreement between
  healthcare providers and parents, or when parental decisions
  are not in the child's best interest, legal intervention may be
  necessary. Courts can appoint guardians or make decisions to
  protect the child's welfare.

Confidentiality and Privacy

Maintaining confidentiality and privacy in pediatric care is essential,
with specific considerations for adolescent patients.

- Health Information Privacy: Compliance with laws such as
  the Health Insurance Portability and Accountability Act
  (HIPAA) in the U.S. ensures that patient information is
  protected.
- Adolescent Confidentiality: Respecting the confidentiality of
  adolescent patients, particularly concerning sensitive issues
  like sexual health or substance use, is important while
  balancing parental rights to information.

End-of-Life Decisions

End-of-life decisions in pediatric care are particularly challenging,
requiring sensitivity and adherence to ethical and legal standards.

- Advance Directives: While rare in pediatrics, advance directives and discussions about end-of-life preferences can be relevant for adolescents with chronic or terminal conditions.
- Do Not Resuscitate (DNR) Orders: DNR orders must be carefully considered, clearly documented, and regularly reviewed, ensuring alignment with the child's and family's wishes and best interests.

EFFECTIVE COMMUNICATION

Shared Decision-Making

Shared decision-making involves collaboration between healthcare providers, patients, and families to make informed and respectful decisions.

- Building Trust: Establishing trust through empathy, active listening, and clear communication is fundamental.
- Providing Support: Offering emotional and psychological support to families during decision-making processes helps them cope with the stress and complexity of medical decisions.

Cultural Sensitivity

Cultural sensitivity is crucial in pediatric care, recognizing and respecting the diverse cultural backgrounds of patients and their families.

- Cultural Competence: Healthcare providers should strive to understand cultural beliefs and practices that influence healthcare decisions, ensuring respectful and appropriate care.
- Interpreter Services: Providing interpreter services for non-English speaking families is essential for effective communication and informed consent.

CASE STUDIES AND APPLICATIONS

Ethical Dilemmas in Neonatal Care

Case studies highlighting ethical dilemmas in neonatal care can provide practical insights and guidance for healthcare providers.

Case Study: Extreme Prematurity: Discussing the ethical considerations in deciding the extent of interventions for extremely premature infants, including long-term prognosis and quality of life.

Case Study: Genetic Disorders: Exploring the ethical and legal issues in managing neonates with severe genetic disorders, balancing the potential for meaningful life with the burdens of treatment.

Legal Challenges in Pediatric Respiratory Care

Examining legal challenges and precedents in pediatric respiratory care can inform best practices and policy development.

Case Study: Parental Refusal of Treatment: Analyzing cases where parents refuse recommended treatments, the legal processes involved, and outcomes.

Case Study: Resource Allocation: Reviewing legal and ethical aspects of resource allocation during critical care situations, such as during pandemics or resource shortages.

Navigating ethical and legal issues in neonatal and pediatric respiratory care requires a thorough understanding of ethical principles, legal frameworks, and effective communication strategies. By fostering trust, ensuring informed and shared decision-making, and respecting cultural diversity, healthcare providers can deliver compassionate and equitable care. Continual education and reflection on these issues are essential for advancing pediatric respiratory care and safeguarding the rights and well-being of young patients.

DISCUSSION QUESTIONS

How can healthcare providers balance the ethical principles of autonomy and beneficence when making decisions about complex pediatric respiratory care?

What are the legal implications of parental refusal of recommended treatment in pediatric respiratory care, and how should such situations be handled?

CONCLUSION

The journey through this book has illuminated the multifaceted world of neonatal and pediatric respiratory care, highlighting the intricate physiological dynamics, diverse range of disorders, and evolving landscape of treatments and technologies. As healthcare providers, researchers, and policymakers, our commitment to advancing pediatric respiratory care involves staying informed about the latest developments, embracing new technologies, and continually refining our approaches to treatment and management.

Adopting a patient-centered approach, fostering effective communication, and upholding ethical standards will ensure that we not only meet the clinical needs of our young patients but also support their overall well-being and quality of life.

By integrating multidisciplinary perspectives, embracing innovation, and addressing the ethical and legal challenges that arise, we can continue to make significant strides in providing exceptional care for neonates and children with respiratory conditions.

REFERENCES

- American Academy of Pediatrics (AAP). (2020). *Neonatal Resuscitation Textbook*
- Centers for Disease Control and Prevention (CDC). (2021). *Vaccines and Immunizations.*
- Fanaroff, A. A., & Martin, R. J. (2019). *Neonatal-Perinatal Medicine: Diseases of the Fetus and Infant.*
- Kliegman, R. M., et al. (2020). *Nelson Textbook of Pediatrics.*
- National Institutes of Health (NIH). (2021). *Respiratory Syncytial Virus (RSV).*
- Pediatric Acute Lung Injury and Sepsis Investigators (PALISI) Network. (2021). *Advances in Pediatric Acute Respiratory Distress Syndrome.*
- Rogers, M. C., et al. (2018). *Textbook of Pediatric Intensive Care.*
- Thébaud, B., et al. (2019). *Stem Cell Therapy for Bronchopulmonary Dysplasia: An Update. Pediatric Research.*
- World Health Organization (WHO). (2021). *Global Influenza Strategy 2019-2030.*
- Zar, H. J., & Ferkol, T. W. (2014). *The Global Burden of Respiratory Disease—Impact on Child Health. Pediatric Pulmonology.*